The Ball

What is bounced and kicked by people all over the world? It is a soccer ball! Many soccer balls are black and white. Some have patterns. They weigh about as much as a pair of your blue jeans.

Clive Brunskill/AllSport

This is one of the soccer balls that was used at the 1996 Summer Olympics. The Olympics were held in Atlanta, Georgia.

The Field

A soccer field is a rectangle. It can be 100 yards to 130 yards long and 50 yards to 100 yards wide. A jumbo jet could fit inside a soccer field.

Soccer players run up and down the field. They get very few chances to rest. A soccer player can run about eight miles in just one game!

WACKY SOCCER FACTS

To Kick Around

by Sheila Sweeny

Ben Radford/Allsport

This young football player lives in Africa. Football player? Yes, soccer is called football everywhere but in the U.S., Canada, and Australia. Can you guess why it is not called football in the United States? No matter what the sport is called, more than 120 million people around the world play it.

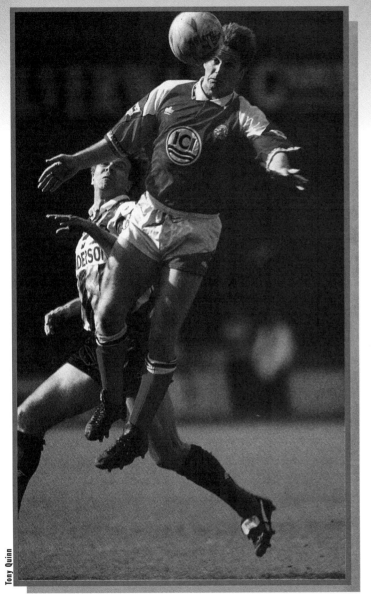

The Players

Each soccer team has 11 players. They try to get the ball into the other team's goal. Players can use almost any part of their body to move the ball. They even use their head!

Only the goalie may use her hands. The goalie tries to keep the ball out of her team's goal.

Soccer Talk

Here are five words and what they mean in soccer:

To **DRIBBLE** means to move the ball by kicking it along the ground.

To **JUGGLE** means to keep the ball in the air by hitting it with any part of the body other than the hands.

A **FORWARD** is a player who tries to score a goal.

A **STRIKER** is a forward whose main job is to score.

A **STOPPER** tries to keep the other team's striker from scoring.

An Old Game

No one knows when the first soccer game was played. But games like soccer have been played for thousands of years.

People in Mexico played games like soccer about 700 years ago. Fans would throw money and jewelry at the winners of the games.

These men are playing a game that is like soccer. It was first played in Italy more than 400 years ago. Today, men play the game once a year. They wear clothes that look like the ones the first players wore. What are they wearing that the first players did not wear?

The World Cup

The World Cup is the biggest event in soccer. It is played every four years. Each country picks its best players to be on its World Cup team.

In 1994, the World Cup took place in the United States. Brazil won. It was Brazil's fourth World Cup win. Brazil has won more World Cups than any other country.

In a 1954 World Cup game, a player lost his shorts. He was scoring a goal when another player ripped off his shorts!

Simon Bruty/Allsport

These fans watched a World Cup game in the U.S. in 1994. Many people came to see the Cup games. A record number of fans watched a World Cup final game in Brazil in 1950. More than 200,000 people were there! Many cities in the United States don't have that many people.

World Cup Players

Pelé *[pay-LAY]* was the best soccer player in the world. Fans called him *O Rei*, which means "The King." Pelé helped Brazil win the World Cup in 1958, 1962, and 1970.

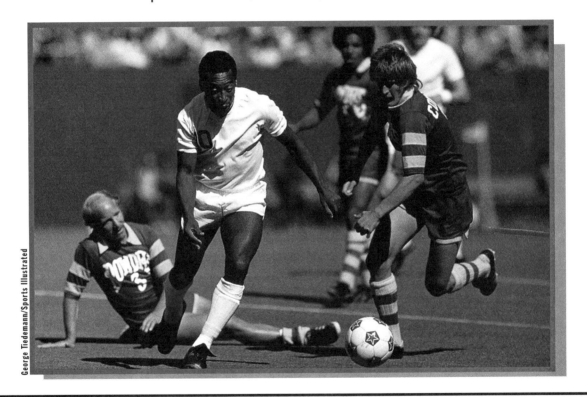

Pelé (white uniform) scored many goals when he played. He once scored eight goals in one game! He was good at everything he did on the field.

Ronaldo de Lima is another great player from Brazil. Ronaldo was 17 years old when he played on Brazil's 1994 World Cup team. Ronaldo plays pro soccer in Europe.

AFP

Major League Soccer

In the United States, many great soccer players play Major League Soccer (MLS). The league began in 1996.

MLS Teams	
Colorado Rapids	Los Angeles Galaxy
Columbus Crew	New England Revolution
D.C. United	New York/New Jersey MetroStars
Dallas Burn	San Jose Clash
Kansas City Wizards	Tampa Bay Mutiny

Tony Quinn/Allsport

Raul Díaz Arce [ARE-say] plays for D.C. United. Raul was the first MLS player to score four goals in one game. He did it in July 1996.

Great MLS Players

Cobi Jones started playing soccer when he was 8 years old. Cobi never dreamed he would play for the U.S. team. Now he plays for the U.S. team *and* the L.A. Galaxy.

Cobi's favorite animal is the hippopotamus. Cobi weighs about 145 pounds. It would take six Cobis to equal the weight of one young hippo!

Alexi Lalas

loved to play both ice hockey and soccer as a kid. Alexi is now a stopper for the U.S. team and the New England Revolution. He also loves to play guitar in a rock band.

Otto Greule/Allsport

15

Women's Soccer

The U.S. women's soccer team is one of the best in the world. The team won a gold medal at the 1996 Olympics. It was the first time women had played soccer in the Olympics.

In 1991, the U.S. team won the first Women's World Championships.

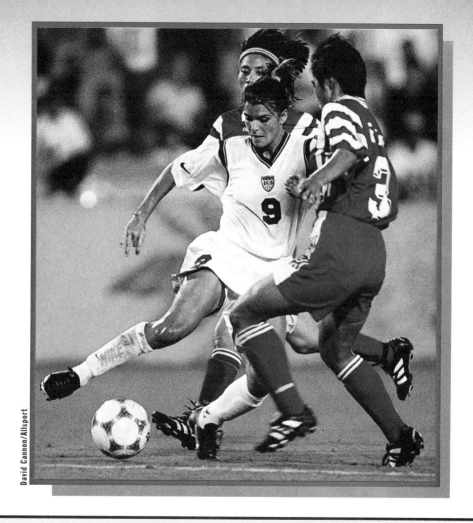

David Cannon/Allsport

Mia Hamm is a striker for the U.S. women's team. She started playing for the team when she was 15. She was the youngest player ever to play for the U.S. team. During the Olympic finals, Mia got hurt. She had to be carried off the field. But Mia was soon smiling. Her team won the gold!

Rain or Shine!

Soccer is played in all kinds of weather. The first MLS championship game was played in heavy rain in 1996.

Simon Bruty/Allsport

Robert Beck

Would you play soccer in your socks? Beach soccer players do. There are five players on each beach soccer team. Players try to keep the ball in the air a lot. That's because you can never tell which way the ball will bounce in the sand.

Long and Far

Do you think you could play soccer for three days without stopping? Twenty-two players in Florida did that. Their soccer game lasted 68 hours! It set a world record.

Allan Abuto Nyanjong
[oh-BOO-toe NYAWN-jong] is a world-record soccer-ball juggler. He kept a ball in the air for more than half a day. He bounced the ball about 98,800 times!

How far could you dribble a soccer ball? Two college students dribbled a soccer ball 100 miles. They kicked the ball from Princeton, New Jersey, to New York City and back. It took 49 hours to make the trip.

Soccer Fans

Rick Stewart/Allsport

Soccer fans cheer. They shout. They cry. Some fans paint their faces and bodies. Others dress in funny costumes. But all these fans have one thing in common: They love soccer!

More people around the world watch soccer on TV than watch any other sport. About two billion people watched the 1994 World Cup final. That means more than one out of every three people in the world was watching!

The fans of D.C. United like to be heard. They stomp and jump. In 1996, they did it so much that they made parts of the stadium move!

Fancy Fans

Some players have their own fans. Carlos Valderrama plays for the Tampa Bay Mutiny. Fans love his big bushy hair. In 1997, there was a Carlos Valderrama Wig Night. The Mutiny handed out 5,000 wigs. Many fans looked like Carlos!

Stephen Dunn/Allsport

Joe Ciblin/Allsport

Carlos is captain of the Mutiny. He grew up in Colombia. That is a country in South America. Can you find Colombia on a globe?

Carlos has a nickname. It is **El Pibe** [PEE-bay]. It means "The Kid" in Spanish.

Soccer Kids

Who loves soccer? Kids do! Almost three out of every four Americans who play soccer are under the age of 18. What is your favorite sport?

Rick Stewart/Allsport

Abigail McGahan was a soccer player in England. The boys on her team wouldn't pass her the ball. So Abigail decided to become a soccer referee! At the age of 12, she passed all the tests you have to take to become a referee. But Abigail had to wait to turn 14 to get on the field and referee adult games.

USA Cup

Every year, some of the world's best young soccer players travel to Blaine, Minnesota. They play in the USA Cup. Some 13,000 kids from 22 countries play in the USA Cup.

The USA Cup is played at the
National Sports Center, in Minnesota.
It has more than 50 soccer fields!
It is the biggest soccer complex
in the world.

Phil Stephens

The Tokyo Fuchu Thunder (in white) traveled more than 5,000 miles to compete in the USA Cup. The Andover Invaders (in blue) only had a 10-minute drive to the game.

Kick It!

S. Indermaur/Allsport

People all over the world get a kick out of soccer. In fact, someone somewhere is kicking a soccer ball right now. Is it you?

THINGS TO DO

WITH

VIKINGS

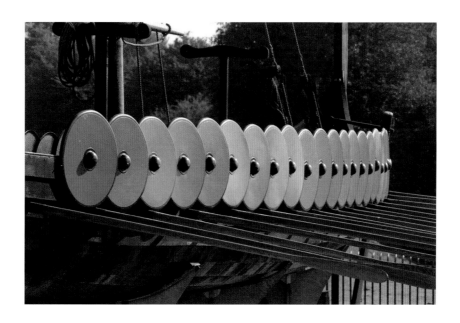

SARA GOODWINS

Loaghtan Books
Caardee
Dreemskerry Hill
Maughold
Isle of Man
IM7 1BE

Published by Loaghtan Books

First published: August 2014

Typesetting and origination by:
Loaghtan Books

Printed and bound by:
Lavenham Press

Website: www.loaghtanbooks.com

ISBN: 978 1 908060 10 5

Photographic copyright © George Hobbs, 2014
unless otherwise stated

For Irene Spiers
whose idea this was

Front cover: Breckon, *Up Helly Aa, Shetland,* © *David Gifford Photography*

Rear cover: Viking ship, ancient symbol of Mann, St Adamnan's Church, Lonan, Isle of Man

Title and contents pages: Detail of Viking ship Hugin, *Pegwell Bay, Kent, England*

CONTENTS

WHERE DID THE VIKINGS COME FROM?

Vikings lived in the far north of Europe in what is now Norway, Sweden, Denmark and parts of Finland. They are often known as Norsemen, which means 'people from the North', and were descended from people who had lived in what is now Germany, but who moved north after the last ice age. The Romans knew of the Norse lands but, as with the Isle of Man and Scotland, never invaded or ruled Scandinavia, although they did trade with Viking merchants. The Viking lands were cold, harsh and a long way from the rest of Europe so were difficult to get to. As a result the Norsemen were relatively isolated until something made them start to attack their neighbours.

Left: the head of Odin's Raven, the longship in the House of Manannan, Peel, Isle of Man
Right: The Viking Raiders Stone, Lindisfarne, England. Thought to be a memorial of the first Viking raids in 793, it marked a grave and shows a line of men holding swords and an axe

DID YOU KNOW?

Vikings travelled as far as Constantinople (now Istanbul) to trade with merchants from the Far East. They got there by travelling from Finland along the rivers of mainland Europe.

ISLE OF MAN

100th anniversary king magnus haraldson

isle of man

793

Raid on Lindisfarne and Jarrow, Northumberland, England is the first Viking raid on western Europe

HOW DID THEY TRAVEL...?

Most people know that Vikings are superb sailors. They probably developed the skill because the Scandinavian coast is very bitty, with coves, bays, inlets and small islands all over the place. With mountains inland, anyone wanting to travel would find it easier to go by sea.

The earliest Viking ships were around 22 metres long – about the same length as two buses parked end to end – just over 5 metres wide and needed a crew of probably no more than about 30. Each ship had a sail about 90 square metres – roughly the same size as a classroom– which was woven from homespun wool on the same looms the women used to weave cloth for clothing. The lengths of cloth were therefore quite narrow and were often dyed before being sewn together, so the sail would probably have been striped. The ship carried around 15 pairs of oars for additional speed, and for when the wind wasn't blowing

Viking ship Hugin, *Pegwell Bay, Kent, England*

in the direction they wanted. Speeds of 25 knots (25 nautical miles per hour) were possible but longships probably cruised at no more than 15 knots – say at about the same speed as the trams on the Manx Electric Railway. Swedes settled along the west coast of Scotland, and Danes in north and west England, but most of the Vikings who came to Mann sailed from Norway. Even in good weather the voyage around the top of Scotland would probably take around four to five days.

Fast and manoeuvrable for raiding, longships were big enough to carry plunder from raids away with them. Some longships didn't need much more than about a metre of water to be able to float, so they could travel inland along rivers. When he wanted to become king of the Isle of Man, Godred Crovan sailed three kilometres up the Sulby River from the coast at Ramsey. Better known as King Orry he and his 300 men defeated King Fingal at the battle at Sky Hill in 1079 to become King of Mann.

They might have been the Ferraris of the seas, but the longships were not luxurious for a crew who would be spending several days and nights on board. The deck was completely open, so if it rained or the sea was rough everything got wet. The crew slept on the planking in hide sleeping bags made with the fur on the inside for warmth, and the leather on the outside to be partially waterproof. Food would have been dried or smoked

DID YOU KNOW?

Travelling overland was easier in winter when the cold weather froze the ground allowing skis, skates and sledges to be used.

Vikings reach the Irish Sea and attack St Patrick's Isle, Isle of Man. Also reach the Bay of Biscay north of Spain

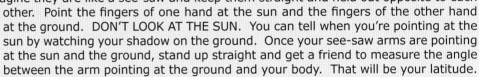

HAVE A GO AT VIKING NAVIGATION

Vikings needed to know how far north or south they were (their latitude), in order to sail where they wanted to go, safely.

First you need to find out where north is. At night look for the pattern of stars called the plough and use it to find the north or pole star. During the day or when it's cloudy hang a lodestone, which is a naturally magnetic rock – they are often found on beaches in Norway and Sweden, and were also in the mines at Maughold, Isle of Man – on a piece of string. Providing the stone is not too heavy it will swing towards north.

Now you need to find how far away from the north you are. When the sun is highest in the sky (midday during the winter, 1.00 pm during British Summer Time) stand up straight and put your arms out at shoulder level; imagine they are like a see-saw and keep them straight and held out opposite to each other. Point the fingers of one hand at the sun and the fingers of the other hand at the ground. DON'T LOOK AT THE SUN. You can tell when you're pointing at the sun by watching your shadow on the ground. Once your see-saw arms are pointing at the sun and the ground, stand up straight and get a friend to measure the angle between the arm pointing at the ground and your body. That will be your latitude.

At night, point your see-saw arms at the north star; as the north star doesn't move you can do this whenever you can see the stars. This time your friend will need to measure the angle between the ground and your outstretched arm; it will be the same as the angle you measured in daylight between your body and your outstretched arm. Use a piece of string or even kneel down to make it easier.

Vikings may have used a stick, their fingers or perhaps even the mast of their ship – all you need is a vertical with a moveable cross piece. Once they knew their latitude and which way was north, they knew which way to go.

meat or fish which would have been taken onto the ship in tubs. Ships would also have carried fresh water and possibly milk or small (weak) ale.

On a ship, particularly on a long voyage, it's easy to get out of sight of land. To avoid getting lost, Vikings worked out where they were by watching the sea currents, marine animals and birds, clouds and driftwood, the wind and the sky. Of these the only one which doesn't change too much is the sky, specifically the sun, moon and stars. Working out how far north you are (latitude) is much easier than working out how far east or west you are (longitude). Fortunately, from the Viking point of view, it was also more important; if they were blown off course, provided they got back to the right latitude they could sail directly east or west and be bound to end up where they wanted to be.

Some people also think that Vikings had technology to help with navigation; some things have been found which don't seem to have any other explanation. Such equipment includes charts or tables saying where a ship should be at certain latitudes, lodestones (magnetic rocks) to find north, and crystals or 'sunstones' which polarise daylight (split it into two) so that navigators know the direction the light is coming from and therefore where the sun is, even when it's cloudy. Technology which can be used in the daytime is very important as there is very little darkness during the summer, so the stars are not very useful. Vikings may also have used a bearing dial (bearing meaning which way you are going, not how much you are carrying) which was a notched wooden dial, although we're not quite sure how it worked.

Vikings establish a permanent base on the Isle of Man from which to raid the surrounding islands

At the beginning, Vikings raided for plunder, pure and simple. This could be gold and silver, jewellery, tools, wool and leather, food, animals and even people, which they took as slaves. Anything valuable and portable. Not only was raiding a 'get rich quick' activity, Vikings also considered it a suitably heroic and praiseworthy thing to do. Coming home with lots of valuable booty earned the same sort of respect as scoring the winning goal in a cup final.

In fact 'sea warrior' is what the word Viking means, although very few Norsemen were full time raiders. Most were farmers looking to make some money before settling down, or to get the means to feed their family after a bad harvest. They probably thought of 'going Viking' rather like we might think of going to the bank to withdraw savings.

DID YOU KNOW?

Long hair was normal for both men and women, and men also had beards and moustaches. Only thralls or slaves had short hair.

Why Norsemen decided to move permanently to the countries they'd previously robbed is something of a mystery, but it could be precisely because they were farmers. Why bring wealth back when you could just stay where it was? Britain is much warmer than Scandinavia, and has lots of rain, so farms were richer and more fertile than the Norsemen had at home. In the middle of the Irish Sea, the Isle of Man was not only good farming country, it also provided an excellent strategic base from which to raid the islands around it. The Vikings knew that the people who lived there were no match for them in a fight. After only a few years of pillaging the raiders became the invaders.

Viking ship, Dim Riv *('daybreak'), off Lerwick, Shetland. The Isle of Bressay is in the background*

861
Vikings discover Iceland

VIKING NAMES

DID YOU KNOW?

Four of the names for the days of the week come from Norse, the language of the Vikings:

Tuesday or Týr's Day. Týr or Tiw is a god of war and noted for courage.
Wednesday or Odin's Day. Odin or Óðin is the leader of the gods and also a god of war.
Thursday or Thor's Day. Thor or Þór is god of thunder and Odin's son.
Friday or Freyja's Day. Freyja – the name means 'lady' in Old Norse – is the goddess of love, beauty and fertility.

For Vikings, names were very important. Giving a child a name meant that it was accepted into the family, while the choice of name represented their character and so was an important part of who they were. Children were often named after grandparents or other close relatives who had died, as Viking's believed that the skills and gifts of the relative would inspire similar characteristics in the child who had been given their name.

As names were considered so important, naming a child was a special occasion. The baby would be washed and dressed and then put on the floor at the feet of their father. When its father picked the baby up, he was agreeing to make sure it had all it needed to grow and be healthy. The child was also sprinkled with water and given gifts by other members of its family.

Children in Viking families didn't have the same surname as their mother and father. Children took their second name from the first name of one of their parents, usually their father. Surnames such as Davidson ('son of David') and Kelly (from MacCeallaigh, 'Ceallach's son') do the same thing today. So a boy called Steven (*Svein* 'young man') whose father was Harold (*Harald* 'army leader'), would be Svein Haraldson. Catherine (*Katrín* 'cheerful') whose father was Eric (*Eirik* 'unique prince') might be Katrín Eiriksdotter. Just as we might shorten Jennifer to Jenny, Vikings also shortened names, so *Katrín* could become *Kata*.

Vikings loved giving each other nicknames, although not usually to people's faces – unless of course the nickname was complimentary in some way. Nicknames could arise from all sorts of things, but were often made up from skills, physical appearance, behaviour and prowess (or otherwise!) in battle.

SOME VIKING NICKNAMES

Harald Fairhair – First King of Norway c. 858; the Isle of Man was ruled from Norway at the time. Presumably he was unusually blond.

Eirik Bloodaxe – Son of Harald Fairhair, also King of Norway and Mann. He got his nickname because he killed his half-brothers to inherit the throne.

Harald Greycloak – Son of Eirik Bloodaxe, King of Norway (and Mann) from 933. Was called Greycloak because he and his followers all wore grey cloaks made in Iceland.

Godred Crovan – King of Mann, Dublin, Leinster and parts of Scotland. Known in Mann as King Orry. Crovan means 'white hand'.

Magnus Barelegs – King Magnus III of Norway, Mann and the Isles from 1098. He got his name from his habit of wearing a tunic without the leggings which would normally have gone underneath it.

The Voyage of "Odin's Raven"
27th May – 4th July 1979
ISLE OF MAN 15P

880
Treaty of Wedmore divides England giving the south and west to Alfred the Great of Wessex and subjecting the north and east to Danelaw, i.e. Viking rule

HOW DID THEY LIVE?

Viking houses were rectangular and usually about 30 to 60 metres long – about twice the length of a longship – and so are called longhouses. The bottom of the walls were built using stone to provide good foundations and to stop the rest of the wall from rotting. On top of the stone base the walls could be made of more stone, or wooden planks, logs, a mud and straw mix called wattle and daub, or turf. The pitched roof was covered with either turf or thatch. Frequently the walls of longhouses curved slightly outwards from either end, so that they were wider in the middle, possibly to leave room for the fireplace. The remains of the longhouses at The Braaid, Marown, Isle of Man bulge outwards in the middle in this way.

Reconstructed Viking longhouse at Brookpoint, Unst, Shetland, built using traditional Viking techniques © Shetland Amenity Trust

Just like today, the exact design of the longhouse differed according to where the house was and what the Vikings had to build with – and quite possibly what different builders preferred. In the north, where there are fewer trees, most of the wall might be built of stone (see picture) or turf. Further south where there were more trees, the walls were made of wood, which was quicker to use but didn't last as long.

The big difference from the way we live today is that several Viking families, who were usually related, lived together in one house – a bit like rooms in a hotel, but with no interior walls. The earth floor of the longhouse was hammered flat and then spread with ashes from the fire, partly to soak up damp and partly to provide some protection against insects such as fleas. Longhouses usually had no windows and light came from the fire, or from pottery lamps using fish oil. Or of course by leaving the door open! Doors, by

885
Norsemen besiege Paris, France

the way, were wooden and hung on hinges often made of leather. In the middle of the floor was a hearth made of a circle of stones; the smoke from the fire escaped through a vent hole in the roof.

The fire provided light, warmth and somewhere to cook food. Fire was started by striking something iron (often made for the purpose and called a firesteel)

Above: the 'hogback' warrior tomb, St Mary's Church, Gosforth, Cumbria, England. Carved by Norsemen it is shaped like a Viking longhouse © Terry Staniforth
Right: the remains of the Viking longhouse at The Braaid, Marown, Isle of Man. It might once have looked something like the carving above

Millennium of Tynwald

10th Century Meeting of Tynwald

7p ISLE OF MAN

J.H.NICHOLSON R.I.   1979   WADDINGTON

against a stone (often flint). This made sparks which fell onto a piece of cloth soaked in fish oil or animal fat. The cloth began to smoulder, the firelighter blew on it and, hey presto, a fire! Flint is found in limestone, which can be found in many places in Britain including North Wales, the North Pennines and Northumberland in England, and around Castletown on the Isle of Man. Vikings would have carried the materials for lighting fires in a pouch hung from a leather belt, rather like matches in a box.

c.890
A Viking man is buried at Ballateare, Jurby, Isle of Man

Interior of turf house reconstruction at Eiríksstaðir, Haukadalur, Iceland © hurstwic.org

Along the side walls, between the posts supporting the roof, were a series of raised platforms, like a wide shelf, with wooden partitions dividing the shelf up to make cubicles. Things were stored underneath the platform, while the front part was used as a bench to sit on, eat, talk and work. The back part of the platform was sleeping accommodation. By modern standards the longhouse was quite cramped and some people think that Vikings often slept sitting up.

When they weren't out raiding, the Vikings were farmers, specialising in raising animals more than growing crops. They did grow some crops, such as barley and oats, but not in great quantities, and wheat was a luxury. What was very important was hay to feed their animals through the long, cold, dark winter. Scandinavia has very little daylight in the winter and the Vikings would have brought their habit of cutting and storing hay with them when they moved to new lands. Hay was considered so important that no-one was allowed to neglect land which could grow it. To keep people and animals out of the hay fields so that they wouldn't get trampled, the Vikings built walls round them. Turf was cut

900-960
Most of the Manx crosses are carved and erected

Sandulf cross, St Andrew's Church, Andreas, Isle of Man. Runes at the side of the cross state that 'Sandulf the Black erected this cross to the memory of Arinbjörg his wife'. Some people think that the figure on the horse is Arinbjörg because it's sitting side saddle. Horses were obviously very important

and laid like bricks on top of a stone base. The Manx sod hedges are still built using a variation of the Viking technique. They are usually about six feet high and six wide, and made from two dry stone walls built next to each other. The two walls are built and then the core is filled with stone and earth. Turf which is cut from land on either side of the wall to make a ditch is then put on top. Prickly bushes such as gorse often grow on top of sod hedges and the whole is almost impossible for animals to get through.

Sometimes animals were kept at one end of the longhouse, sometimes in separate buildings. At The Braaid, Marown, Isle of Man, the smaller of the longhouses was probably a cattle byre. The walls don't curve to leave room for a fire, there are no signs of raised benches and the inside partitions are of slate and divide off areas roughly the size of stalls.

Cows were probably the most important domestic animals for Vikings. A man's wealth was judged by the number of cows he owned or could buy

and Vikings used the same word, *fé*, to mean both wealth and cattle. The same thing still happens in some places today. In Botswana, Africa, people who own a lot of cattle are thought rich, while in Scandinavia it's considered very rude to ask a Sami reindeer herder how many animals he owns, as it's like asking how much money he has in the bank.

Owning horses was a status symbol – rather like owning a posh car. Viking horses were similar to the Icelandic horses of today, 13-14 hands (about 4½ feet tall) with a thick coat and hardy enough to stand cold winters outside.

Sheep were important providers of wool, meat and milk, particularly wool, so it's a little odd that shepherding was not considered a respectable job for a Viking man. The Gute is the oldest breed of sheep found in

DID YOU KNOW?

Vikings grew vegetables such as carrots, parsnips, beans, peas and onions, as well as flax to make linen.

A Manx loaghtan sheep

Scandinavia and is thought to be the breed which the Norsemen would have known and farmed. The sheep were small, hardy, and could be a mixture of white, brown, grey or black, and often had four horns. Vikings are credited with introducing the Gute sheep to the Isle of Man where it developed into the Loaghtan. The two breeds remained very similar until about three hundred years ago when the Loaghtan was bred to favour the brown colouring. In the early twentieth century the same thing happened to the Gute only it was bred to be grey. The Loaghtan and Gute shed their wool and Viking women and children would have gathered the

Above: the cattle byre at The Braaid, Marown, Isle of Man
Right: a traditional Manx sod hedge, Maughold, Isle of Man

wool from hedges and fields.

Vikings would also have kept goats and possibly pigs, although they were considered messy and difficult to control. Dogs certainly guarded Viking farms, while cats kept mice away from stored grain.

VIKING PLACE NAMES

Many places are still called by their Viking name, at least in part:

'Aa' is 'river', so we have Cornaa (corn river), Laxey (salmon river) and Ramsey (wild garlic river).
'Byr' or 'by' is 'farm', so we have Crosby (cross farm), Dalby (dale farm) and Grenaby (green farm).
'Eyrr' is 'gravel bank', so we have Point of Ayre (the point of the gravel bank) and Lezayre (of the gravel bank).
'Nes' is 'nose', so Langness is 'long nose'.
'Vík' is creek, so Garwick is 'spear creek'.

937
Athelstan of Wessex defeats Norse, Scots and north Welsh at Brunanburh (probably somewhere near the Wirral) making him King of England and Scotland. Some Viking refugees arrive on the Isle of Man after the battle

DON'T FORGET THE GIRLS!

As some societies still do today, Vikings divided tasks fairly strictly into what men and women were allowed to do. Women didn't automatically have to do what men told them to, however. Who made the decisions tended to change whether you were inside or outside the home. Women decided what happened inside; men decided what happened outside.

Men were farmers, raiders and warriors – women were not allowed to fight or wear men's clothing – took part in politics and arranged the laws. Women ran the house (and the farm if the men were away), were in charge of the family's money, looked after the children and were nurses and healers. Often healing involved using magic, which was considered dishonourable for men.

Viking men quarrelled among themselves, but Viking law said that women had a right not to be pestered by men. Presumably such laws only applied to Vikings as women could be captured as slaves. Women could own their own property and, if their marriage wasn't working, could divorce their husbands but expect him still to provide for their children.

Because women looked after the house they were responsible for preparing food – which included milking the animals, gathering berries and cooking – storing food for the winter and making clothes. In fact making, cleaning and handling clothes were considered so much women's work that a woman could sometimes stop a man going out by covering his weapons with clothing. Not only would a man not think of going anywhere without at least a knife – it would be like going out without your trousers today – but he would be very reluctant even to pick up the clothing in order to move it. How many men today would like to be seen carrying a woman's handbag?

Norwegian Forest Cat, Norsvana Sugar Sparkle. © Tracy and Colin Wood. Norsvana Norwegian Forest Cats, North Yorkshire

Although not taking part in raiding, some women were involved in exploration. Vikings moving to new lands might take their wives with them, or might marry local girls. Just like today, wedding gifts would often be something useful for their new home, but newly married girls might also be given a cat to keep mice out of stored food. Viking pest control! The cat probably most familiar to Vikings was the *Norsk Skogkatt* (sometimes spelt *skaukatt*) or Norwegian Forest cats.

> **DID YOU KNOW?**
>
> Viking women are not called Viqueens. (Pity really!)

WHAT DID VIKINGS WEAR?

It's cold in Scandinavia so Vikings wore a lot of wool to keep warm They also used some linen, and anyone rich could buy silk from traders. Women spent a lot of time making first yarn, then cloth and then clothing. Historians estimate that it takes about a week's worth of spinning to make enough yarn for one day's weaving. A Viking weaver could weave about half a square metre of cloth per day and it takes about one and a half square metres of cloth to make a pair of trousers. That's a total of roughly four weeks work full time. At the age of about four girls were taught to spin using a simple drop spindle consisting mainly of a large stone with a hole in it, which was called a 'spindle whorl' (see page 18). Small strands of wool are tied to the stone through the hole, the stone is dangled from the wool, spun gently and so twists the strands of wool into yarn. The weight of the stone keeps the yarn straight and taut, and the twist gives it strength. Often a stick is inserted into the central hole partly to make the spinning easier and faster, and partly

> **DID YOU KNOW?**
>
> Both men and women carried personal combs. Men usually had a comb case made from bone or antler to protect their comb from damage. Women are thought to have carried their combs inside a cloth pouch.

to provide somewhere for the spinner to wind the new yarn onto.

Once there was enough, the yarn was either woven on a loom to make cloth, or turned into small garments like hats or socks, by a process called *nålebinding*. Although knitting has been around since about 1100, it was invented in the Middle East, possibly in Egypt, and hadn't got as far north as the Vikings. They developed their own way of looping yarn to make things. *Nålebinding* means 'nail binding'; the nail is what we would call a needle. Some people call it Viking knitting.

Above and left: clothing typical of that worn by men and women throughout the Norse regions, modelled by members of Hurstwic. The group's main focus is to research and practice Viking-age fighting moves as explained in the Sagas of Iceland and elsewhere. Photographs © hurstwic.org

c. 950
Gautr Björnsson, Viking mason named on crosses in Kirk Michael and Andreas was carving Manx crosses

One of a pair of oval shoulder broochs which a Viking woman would have used to fasten her overdress (see previous page). This one is on display in Alnwick Castle, Northumberland, England.

Just like today, good clothing made its wearer look important. Men wore trousers underneath a long tunic with a leather belt on top. Cloaks were a large square of woollen cloth, or possibly a whole animal skin, and men would also have worn a woollen or possibly fur hat or hood. Women wore woollen or linen dresses down to their ankles, with a shorter pinafore dress over the top held up by two large oval brooches just below the shoulders. They also wore shawls, braided belts and, if they were married, possibly a linen scarf covering their hair.

We don't know much about Viking underwear but presumably they wore some (or maybe not!). If they did, it was probably made from wool or linen.

Leather, hide and fur was also used to make clothing, particularly for men. Men hung a leather pouch and a sheath for a knife from their belt; the

MAKE YOUR OWN VIKING BEANIE

Nålebinding is a bit like tatting, or a mixture of sewing and macramé. It is a series of soft knots made using just your fingers or a blunt needle. Here we've used a needle. Viking needles were made from bone or antler, but a wooden or plastic one works just as well. Because you make things using a lot of knots, whatever you make won't unravel if it gets a hole in it. This makes it very hard wearing, but also makes it difficult to correct mistakes when you're working. Archaeologists have found mittens with mistakes in their working, obviously as a result of the maker not bothering (or not being able) to unknot their wrong work.

There are various stitches, but this is one of the simplest. It's a version of what is sometimes called Oslo stitch, named after a mitten made using this stitch which was found in some excavations in Oslo. Remember that, unlike either knitting or crochet, if you go wrong, pulling the working thread doesn't undo the work, it merely makes the mistake tighter!

1   Cut a length of yarn. Tie a loose knot in one end and thread a blunt needle through the other end. Don't tie the knot too tight as you'll need to get your needle through it later.

2   *Insert the needle into the knot from the front and over the top of the working yarn. Don't pull the loop too tight as you'll need to get your needle through it later.

3   Repeat from * until the original knot has a lot of loops around it.

Penannular brooch often worn in a cloak. The pin passes through the cloth and then turns on the ring to hold the material securely. This is a modern copy.

knife was used for eating with as well as fighting. When going Viking they might also have carried a sword in a leather sheath and be wearing a leather battle helmet. Metal helmets were showier and better protection but also more expensive. Boiled leather gives very good protection against injury; even Second World War bomb disposal teams sometimes wore leather jerkins as body armour. Fur from animals such as squirrels, seals, bears and even cats was used for warmth and decoration.

Nowadays we're not used to thinking of clothing as wealth, but only rich Vikings had spare clothing. It was considered a mark of someone's status if visitors arrived wet from the rain, and were offered dry clothing to change into.

4   At the start of the second round, insert the needle into the front of the loop of the first of the stitches and over the top of the working yarn as usual.

5   † Insert the needle into the front of the loop of the stitch below and into the back of the loop of the previous stitch. Keep the working yarn on the left of the needle and pull through; this is why you mustn't tighten the yarn too much or the needle will not pass through previous loops smoothly. The working yarn then becomes the loop through which you will pass the needle next time.

6   Repeat from †.

7   If you want to make the circle bigger then put the needle twice into the front of the same stitch. To shape the circle or disk into a bowl or hat then don't take any extra stiches and the diameter of the circle will remain the same. As you work your additional stitches will gradually form a dish and then a bowl (or hat!).

8   To make a hat you will need to increase the circle until it is about the same size as the crown of your head before beginning to shape the bowl. Viking women would have tried their work on the head of the person the hat was being made for. If you try it on as you go, then you can increase the size by adding stiches/loops or not as required. When you run out of yarn just knot the next length on. Vikings would have spliced or felted the two together, but knotting is easier when you're learning.

c.980
The round tower is built on St Patrick's Isle, Peel, Isle of Man

Both men and women liked wearing jewellery. Men held their cloaks in place with elaborate pins, and rich men and women both wore heavy armlets and torcs (solid metal bands worn around the arm or neck, with a gap in them so that wearers could get them on and off). A hoard of Viking jewellery and coins was found in 1894 when builders were digging the foundations for 66 Derby Road, Douglas, Isle of Man. Most of them are now in the British Museum but some were returned to the Manx Museum.

Women also prized strings of beads. Beads were expensive so women hung them between the large shoulder brooches which held up their dress. That way women needed fewer beads to be eye-catching, than if they were worn as a necklace. One of the richest tenth-century female graves known outside Scandinavia was found in 1984 during an archaeological excavation on St Patrick's Isle, Peel, Isle of Man. Now known as The Pagan Lady, the grave's occupant had with her seventy-three high-quality beads (see stamp on previous page) the largest nearly four centimetres in diameter. The large beads may even have doubled as spindle whorls. Viking ladies often kept things they valued such as spindle whorls, keys and firesteels hanging from their belt, or among their beads – we might do the same with a mobile phone today. Displayed hanging from a belt such things were handy, looked good and showed off their owner's wealth. Boasting was important to Vikings.

Viking spindle whorls on display in Alnwick Castle, Northumberland, England. These are about 3cm in diameter. The top one is made of stone, the bottom three of bone. Such items were often worn as jewellery when not in use.

St Olave, St Olave's Church, Ramsey, Isle of Man. The stained glass is lovely, but the saint's clothing is a Victorian idea of what Vikings might have worn and is almost entirely wrong!

983-5
Eric the Red explores Greenland and establishes small settlements there

WHAT DID THEY EAT?

Vikings used the same word, *fé*, to mean both cattle and money. Cows were very important to Vikings as they provided many of the things Vikings ate, including milk, butter, cheese and *skyr*, which looks like a thick yoghurt but is actually a fermented soft cheese. *Skyr* is made from skimmed milk, after the cream has been taken off to make butter, so it has little fat, but lots of protein. It is also delicious. Cows stop producing milk in the winter so, because *skyr* doesn't go off, it became the Vikings' main source of dairy food during the dark months.

Keeping grazing animals over winter needs a lot of hay, so many of the male animals would have been allowed to mate and then have been killed for meat. Viking farms produced beef, mutton, goat, pork and also horsemeat. When the Norsemen became Christian, the church didn't like people eating horsemeat so it faded from the diet. Vikings also kept chickens, geese and ducks partly for their eggs and partly to eat. Meat was often boiled in large iron cauldrons or cooked above the fire on a spit as a kind of Viking barbecue. It could also be roasted in soapstone pots. Soapstone is very common in Finland and is a soft stone which Vikings used to carve into cooking pots as they had very few pots made out of clay.

Eating only meat or fish isn't healthy. While the men were off hunting, the women and children gathered berries, wild plants, herbs, fruit and even seaweed. Apples, pears, sloes, plums, blackberries, strawberries, raspberries and bilberries were all found growing wild, as were hazelnuts, although they were not all found everywhere. Norsemen were also gardeners and grew vegetables including carrots, parsnips, turnips, cabbage, celery, radishes, beans, peas, mushrooms and leeks. Barley, rye and oats were used for making bread, and barley and oats were cooked in water or milk to make a sort of porridge. Honey was used to sweeten food, and herbs such as mustard and horseradish provided extra flavour. Like we do today, Vikings also imported foods they particularly liked, such as walnuts, wine and figs.

Although they got most of their meat from their farms, Vikings hunted animals such as deer, squirrel, hare, whale and seal – although whales were rarely hunted at sea and most whale meat came from animals which had swum onto beaches by mistake. Vikings made the most of any animal they killed, eating the meat, cooking with the fat, and using the skin or fur as clothing. In addition they also used whale and seal oil for lighting lamps and sometimes used the blubber as a substitute for butter. Nor surprisingly, as they were such good seamen, Vikings were also good fishermen, both with a rod and line, and with nets. They also collected shellfish and the eggs of sea birds, and caught and ate the birds themselves.

In order to keep food for the winter, meat, fish and vegetables were smoked or dried in the sun, or were pickled in the whey from milk. In northern Scandinavia, where it's very cold, Vikings packed ice around their meat to freeze it. They also fermented meat by packing a prepared carcass into a pit lined with grass, covering it to keep out oxygen, and leaving it for several weeks. The result can be delicious, but it's risky and can result in bad meat or food poisoning. Food was also occasionally salted using salt made by boiling sea water. Salt was not, however, used as much as you might think, as it required the additional effort of making the salt, before using it to preserve food.

Raiding or invading leaves little time for fancy cookery and one of the main 'packed lunches' for Vikings was dried cod. Because cod contains almost no fat it can be dried hard and will keep almost forever as long as it's kept dry. To use, just add water. It's like a Viking Pot Noodle! Vikings even gnawed on the dried cod fillets if they didn't have time to turn them into soup.

Vikings ate two meals per day, *dagmál* or 'day meal' in the morning and *náttmál* or 'night meal' in the evening. Just like today, what they got to eat depended on what was available and how well off they were.

c.990
Ballafayle hoard is buried near Douglas, Isle of Man

MAKE YOUR OWN VIKING FEAST BREAD

Vikings made porridge or unleavened bread (bread made with flour and water or possibly flour and milk) for ordinary days, but would have made something a little more tasty for celebrations and feast days. Although no Viking recipes survive, the one below uses ingredients which would have been available to Vikings, as well as cooking techniques they would have used. Vikings could therefore have eaten something very similar to this while sitting around the fire in their longhouses, telling stories and having a good time with their friends.

Ingredients
300 g strong wholemeal flour (ordinary plain flour will do, but this is better)
250 ml buttermilk (ordinary full cream milk with a tablespoon of lemon juice also works)
1 small egg (1 egg will do up to four times this amount of dough)
1 tablespoon honey
1 handful chopped nuts (if someone has a nut allergy then use a handful of currants or sultanas instead, but remember that Vikings wouldn't have had that sort of dried fruit)
Small knob of butter for frying (Vikings also used animal fat for frying but butter tastes better!)

Method
Add the buttermilk to the flour (no need to sift the flour!) and mix together with a spoon.
Lightly beat the egg and stir into the flour/milk mixture.
Add the honey and chopped nuts and stir thoroughly; the mixture will be gooey.

Now for the sticky bit! Scoop out enough of the mixture to make a small ball – between the size of a golf ball and a tennis ball. Coat it in flour and flatten it to about 1 cm thick. Repeat until you've used all the mixture; you should have enough for about eight scones.

Melt the butter in a frying pan and add enough breads to cover the bottom of the pan without them touching each other. Don't make the heat too hot or the outside will scorch before the inside is done (it doesn't hurt to eat them before the inside is cooked properly but then they're more like gooey puddings than feast bread and probably not 'Viking'!). When the first side is a mid brown turn the scones over and do the other side for about the same length of time. The cooking should take about four or five minutes each side. You'll know they're done properly if they sound hollow when you tap them.

Eat them warm from the pan and they're delicious. If you let them go cold, or worse still, keep them overnight, they'll go hard.

c. 1000
Viking ship burial takes place at Balladoole, Arbory, Isle of Man

WHAT DID VIKING CHILDREN DO?

Not go to school! Viking children learned from their parents and other older people and, by and large, shared the jobs of the farm. Both sexes were taught how to light and tend a fire, swim, milk animals and grow crops including vegetables. Some jobs such as bird scaring, collecting wood or gathering berries seem to have been done mainly by children, probably because they required no great physical strength.

Girls helped with younger children and were taught how to cook, clean, and run a house and farm. From a very early age they also learned how to spin, weave and make clothing, as the process was very time consuming and their mothers needed all the help they could get. Vikings liked to be well dressed, and some even ironed their clothes. Girls smoothed linen with a large glass pebble on a flat whalebone board. Glass was costly and difficult to make so only the wealthy could afford the luxury of uncreased linen.

Boys were taught all about sailing and fishing, encouraged to wrestle to develop strength and stamina, and trained to fight. Most men fought with an axe, partly because it doubled for use on the farm and partly because that was all they could afford, so boys would probably have been taught axe-fighting skills first. However they would also have been taught at least the basics of how to fight with a knife, sword, spear and bow. Boys may also have been taught how to use a sling shot, but this was more for hunting small animals for the pot than for use in combat. A sling shot could be effective in a fight but its use was considered dishonourable.

Life wasn't all work though, and Viking children rode horses, swam and, when ponds froze, went ice-skating by strapping blades made of bone to their feet. Football wasn't around then, but boys did play a game called *sveinaleikr* – *svein* means 'boy' and *leikr* is a game or match. We

Up Helly Aa, Shetland
© David Gifford Photography

1004
Norse attempt to settle in Newfoundland, Province of Canada, fails

don't now know the rules but *sveinaleikr* was played with balls and sticks and could get rough. Adults had their own version called *knattleikr* (*knatt* means 'knot' and probably referred to the ball). Balls, by the way, were made out of handfuls of wool turned into felt and tied round with twine, the inflated bladders of animals, or animal skins.

Viking children also had toys. Whistles were made from small branches or twigs, often from elder trees. They could also be made from bone, usually from geese. Whistles were either blown or twirled on a string to make a humming noise. Girls had wooden dolls and boys sailed toy boats.

Probably the biggest difference between the life of a modern child and that of a Viking was the system of fostering. Fostering didn't mean that your parents were dead, it meant that you went to stay with a family who could teach you skills your own family didn't have – a bit like going to boarding school. The system of fosterage tended to make Viking society more peaceful as your neighbour would be less likely to quarrel with you if his son lived in your house.

At the age of twelve children were considered adults and by sixteen some were seasoned warriors.

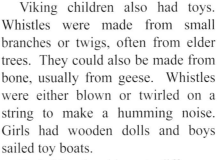

Above and right: Vikings inside and outside the House of Manannan, Peel, Isle of Man. Children wore clothes very similar to those worn by adults and probably cut out of worn out adult clothing

The Mal Lumkun cross in St Michael's Church, Kirk Michael, Isle of Man. The runes on the back say: 'Mal Lumkun erected this cross in memory of Mal Mura his foster [mother]... Better it is to leave a good foster son than a bad son'

1014
Celtic Irish Christians defeat Irish, Manx and Scottish Vikings at the Battle of Clontarf, Dublin, Ireland

VIKING GAMES

Think of Vikings and you think of warriors charging into action, but it's difficult to fight successfully in the dark, and Scandinavia has long dark winters. It's no surprise therefore that Vikings also enjoyed playing games.

Board games were particularly popular, and skilled players were highly respected. Vikings played several board games including a form of backgammon (*kvatrutafl*), fox and geese (*halatafl*) and chess (*skáktafl*). The most popular Viking board game, however, was *hnefatafl*, which probably means 'king's board' and is often called 'game of kings'. *Hnefa* means 'fist' but it usually understood to mean the most important piece, i.e. the king, and *tafl* is table or board.

There are various versions of *hnefatafl* but experts agree that there are always two players. The defending player sets their pieces in the centre of a square board while the attacking player's pieces surround them at the edges. It was a game of strategy and often led to arguments. Boards were made of wood, scratched on skins or even drawn on the ground. The pieces ranged from simple pebbles to highly decorated figures. Some people think that the Lewis chessmen (see picture, right) are really *tafl* pieces. Few boards survive but one of the most complete is about 1,000 years old and was found in 1932 in Ballinderry, West Meath, Ireland. The decoration on it is like that on many of the Manx crosses and has led some experts to suggest that it was made on the Isle of Man.

Vikings also enjoyed a tug of war. Today tug of war contests require two teams to stand facing each other pulling on a rope. The Viking version, *toga hönk* or 'tug loop', was between two people who sat on the floor with the soles of their feet flat against the soles of their opponent's feet. Each opponent held either side of a loop of rope and tried to straighten their legs to pull their opponent over. Just as *hnefatafl* helped players learn how

Above: Viking chess players, Ramsey, Isle of Man. They are shown playing with a set of Lewis chess men (example, left). Dating from the 12th century and discovered on Lewis, Shetland, in the 19th century, the originals were made from walrus ivory and whales teeth

to plan and carry out raids, so *toga hönk* improved the muscles needed for rowing.

Throwing games were also popular, with a version of piggy-in-the-middle played inside a longhouse. Called *skinnleikr* (skin game) because the ball was a rolled up piece of fur, various players threw the fur parcel to each other from the side platforms (see page 11), while someone stood in the middle and tried to jump and catch it.

1025-65
Coins are minted on the Isle of Man from dies (moulds) originally made and used in Ireland

23

SOCIAL ORGANISATION AND VIKING LAW

For people usually considered warlike, Vikings had a huge respect for justice and fairness, and expected most quarrels to be settled according to their local and national laws. They lived in small family communities and so preferred local leaders to a distant king – a parish council rather than a central government. However they also recognised that large issues sometimes needed to be discussed and sorted out, and at those times all free men in the

Tingwall, Shetland

land met to talk about and decide new laws. The meeting was known as a *þing* or *thing* and was the equivalent of the Viking parliament. The old name is still echoed in the names of the parliaments of Iceland (*Althingi*), Norway (*Storting*), Finland (*Lagting*), Denmark (*Folketing*), and the Faroe Isles (*Løgting*). Even Shetland and Orkney had their parliaments, both at places called Tingwall. Tynwald, the Isle of Man's parliament, also gets its name from the old Viking word. The assembly field where a *þing* took place was called the *þing-völlr*, and hence Tynwald. Only in the Isle of Man is the tradition of *þings* unbroken, so Tynwald is the oldest continuous parliament in the world. Vikings invaded the Isle of Man in the early 800s, and *þings* would have been introduced as soon as they settled on the island. Consequently Tynwald has been meeting for more than 1,000 years.

People liked getting together to celebrate midsummer and, to save a lot of travelling, a *þing* was often held at the same time. Tynwald still meets every year on 5 July, old Midsummer's Day. Vikings would recognise a lot of what happens at the modern Tynwald, but Vikings would have had fewer officials.

On Tynwald Day the Lord of Man and Legislative Council (the Manx parliament's upper house) sit on the top level of Tynwald Hill. On the next level down sits the House of Keys, the Manx parliament's lower house. The third level carries representatives from the towns, the police and clergy, while on the lowest tier sit parish captains and the coroners among others.

The tribal chiefs or *goðar* of a Viking *þing* also met on a low hill like Tynwald Hill, so that they could be seen. The mound was linked by a processional way stretching eastwards to a religious and ceremonial site, just as Tynwald Hill is still linked by the processional way to St John's Church.

Vikings included a handful of earth brought from each tribal territory in the *þing* hill, so that everyone there

> **DID YOU KNOW?**
>
> Cairns or piles of rocks were used like signposts. They marked the best route to get to the things and also marked fords in rivers, etc.

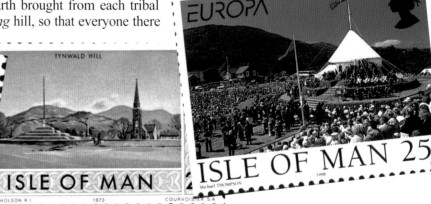

c. 1030
Glenfaba hoard is buried at Poortown near Peel, Isle of Man

could think that they were on their homeground. Viking law stated that you didn't fight your guests! Tynwald Hill is also said to contain earth drawn from each of the seventeen parishes in the island and, even today, part of the ceremony includes symbolically 'fencing' the court. One of the coroners and *Yn Lhaihder* (The Reader) proclaim, the coroner in English and *Yn Lhaihder* in Manx, that no disturbance will be tolerated. Tynwald is then considered protected against attack.

Very little has really changed in the hundreds of years Tynwald has been meeting. The modern *þing* is still held outside (and if it rains, people get wet) and, like the Viking *þing,* sets the laws for the coming year. During the Tynwald ceremony the two deemsters, i.e. the judges, announce all the new laws first in English and then in Manx. At their *þings* Vikings would have been able to complain about problems and get them settled. Anyone living on the Isle of Man today is also entitled to write a 'petition of redress' to present at the foot of Tynwald Hill on Tynwald Day. All petitions must be considered (although not on Tynwald Day) and some have led to a change in Manx law. Even the sideless tent which today shelters the Tynwald dignitaries from the worst of the weather (see stamp on opposite page) can trace its history back to Viking times. Those attending the Viking *þings* would have spent their nights under canvas in *búðir* or portable booths. *Búðir* were tents with roofs made of homespun fabric (like the sails from longships, see page 5). Sometimes the bottom part of a *búðir* was built of stone so that it could be reused year after year. The *þing-völlr* (thing field) would have been a little like a camp-site with on-site facilities.

A few things have changed of course. Only Viking men were allowed to take part in a *þing,* while today women contribute as much as men. The Deemsters now read out the laws, while Viking law speakers would have had to proclaim them from memory. Vikings would also have had to shout while we can use microphones.

One particular part of Tynwald Day would have been very familiar to Vikings. The fair! Vikings would have made the most of any gathering to trade, gossip and have fun.

1035
Danish empire (Denmark, Norway and England) splits up when its ruler King Cnut dies

25

Elves, dwarves and dragons. It sounds like *Lord of the Rings* doesn't it? That's no accident; J.R.R. Tolkein knew a lot about Viking mythology and based his famous book around it.

The Norse gods and goddesses liked war as much as the Vikings did. Several deities had more than one name, so it's difficult to be sure exactly how many Viking gods there were, but probably nearly 200. This was one of the reasons Vikings had no problem accepting Christianity. They just added the Christian God to their list. Very few of the Norse gods were particularly famous and, although their jobs often overlapped,

> **DID YOU KNOW?**
>
> The goddess Freyja rode in a chariot pulled by two wildcats.

many gods were thought to look after aspects of the natural world. Byggvir, for example, was the god of barley, while Ull was the god of frost; he is supposed to have invented skiing.

The main Viking gods included *Óðin* or Odin, who was top god and the god of war, death and knowledge. Then there was his wife Frigg the goddess of the sky and marriage, and their son *Þór* (Thor), god of Thunder (and Thursday). Freyja was also important. As well as being goddess of love and fertility she was also the leader of the Valkyries.

Just as Christianity has angels, Vikings believed in spiritual beings, who were not gods – although, being Vikings, theirs were a lot more warlike. Valkyries, for example, were female warriors who rode howling onto battlefields and carried the men who had been killed to *Valhöll* (Valhalla). The aurora borealis or northern lights are supposed to be caused by the sun glinting off the Valkyries' armour. Valhalla was the Viking heaven and was like one huge party, with lots of feasting, fighting and frolics. People might get hurt but their injuries would heal up overnight.

Vikings don't appear to have had priests, but certain people were religious leaders as well as doing their ordinary job. The closest similarity today are non-stipendiary ministers. The *goðar* or community leaders were probably responsible for conducting public religious ceremonies, while women often performed charms for healing or for keeping their families safe.

The Thorwald cross, St Andrew's Church, Andreas, Isle of Man. The bottom right-hand part of the stone shows the god Týr with the raven of Óðin perched on his shoulder. At his feet is Fenrir the wolf. According to the Norse legends the monster Fenrir was menacing the gods so Týr bound him in fetters. The carving shows Fenrir biting off Týr's right hand, as the god attempts to bind him

c.1050
Most Norsemen have now become Christians and Roolwer, first Bishop of Sodor and Man, is appointed

When important leaders died, they had to be sent to the afterlife correctly. Burial and cremation were both acceptable to Vikings although cremation seems to have been rare in Britain. Really powerful leaders, mostly men but occasionally women, were buried or cremated in ships to show how important they were. Many of the things they'd owned during their lifetime, including animals and even slaves, were often included with them in their last voyage, so that they could be useful in the afterlife.

The man buried in the ship at Balladoole, Arbory, Isle of Man had with him a circular shield, several knives, fire-making equipment, an iron cauldron, stirrups and a horse's bridle and bit, among other things. At his feet lay a female slave. Such a lot of expensive things meant that he was both wealthy and important. A woman was also buried in the grave of a Viking man at Ballateare near Jurby, Isle of Man. She had been killed by being hit on the head. With her in the Ballateare grave were three spears, a knife, sword, scabbard and shield. The shield still showed the patterns of red, white and black painted on it, while the sword was decorated with silver. It had been deliberately broken, possibly to symbolise its master's death.

Vikings also believed in what we would now call zombies. The *draugr* or walking dead were corpses who lived in a burial mound, often beneath a rock, and who wanted to return and interfere with the lives of the people they had left behind. The Ballateare sword may even have been broken so that a *draugr* could not use it.

The Viking ship burial, Balladoole, near Castletown, Isle of Man.
The stones are not original but were set to mark where the Viking ship had lain

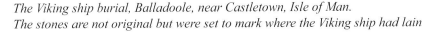

1066
Norsemen are defeated by King Harald at the Battle of Stamford Bridge, Yorkshire, England, and leave English soil

VIKING SAGAS

Quite a lot of what we know about Vikings comes from the long story poems or sagas they left behind. We have to be careful about believing everything that's said in the sagas, however, as that would be like learning about life today from the Harry Potter books. What the sagas are very good at telling us is what Vikings thought was important. For example fighting, feasting and honour are talked about a lot. Women are mentioned very rarely, but when they are, are usually praised for their beauty, feistiness and wisdom.

Gautr's Cross, St Michael's Church, Kirk Michael, Isle of Man. The runes should be read from the bottom upwards and say 'Mail-brikti son of Aþakán smith →

WRITE YOUR NAME IN RUNES

Different countries had slightly different variations of runes, just as, for example, Danish, German and Greek have different alphabets today. Just as the word 'alphabet' comes from the first two Greek letters alpha and beta, so the runic equivalent is known as the futhork from the first six runes in it.

The two main systems are called 'long branch' and 'short twig' because the straight lines used to create the letters are shorter in short twig. Long branch was used in Denmark and Iceland, short twig in Norway, Sweden and the Isle of Man. This is the Manx version of short twig:

ᚠᚢᚦᚭᚱᚴ ᚼᚾᛁᛆᛌᛐᛒᛘᛚᛦᛂ
f u t h o r k h n i a s t b m l R æ

Because Norse had different sounds it didn't necessarily need the same letters as are needed for other languages. Runes were also quite often used back to front or upside down and could be made to be read from right to left.

The runes at the bottom of the stamp on the previous page read 'Maun' which is the Norse name for the Isle of Man.

Anne can be written 'an'

Keith can be written 'kæth'

Try writing your own name.

The sagas are a mix of Viking history, legend and fiction, and were passed on orally, which means that even though they were very long, they were learnt off by heart. A good saga teller was highly respected both as a library of knowledge and as an entertainer. Listening to the sagas was the Viking equivalent of television or the internet.

There were different kinds of saga too. Some were invented as a way of remembering family history, while others passed on knowledge of the law and how Vikings were supposed to behave. Still others told of great national events. Sitting round the fire in your longhouse on a dark winter evening, therefore, you might hear poems about how Gunnar Hámundarson was a spectacular swordsman

1079
Godred Crovan (King Orry) arrives on Mann

Nearly 1,000 years ago (in about 1040) a Viking stonemason called Gautr carved crosses on the Isle of Man. He signed his name (Kaut) in runes at the top of this one, now in St Michael's Church

who got rich by raiding. Or perhaps about how your grandfather walloped your uncle when he came late to the baptism of your mother. Or even about how dew from the giant ash tree Yggdrasil, centre of the universe, supplied mead for Valhalla.

Most of the sagas were not written down until years, sometimes hundreds of years, after they were first told. As a result they gradually changed as different tellers added new stories or left out bits they didn't like or couldn't remember. Although they didn't write down their sagas, the Vikings were not illiterate. Unlike most British peasants at the time, even the very humble could usually read and write. They used runes.

Today runes sound mysterious, but for Vikings runes were just their alphabet. In their language the word 'rune' meant letter or text. They put runes on everything. A comb case found in Lincoln, Eng-

Above: runes used as a modern decoration on Skandia House, Douglas, Isle of Man. They are in fact a simple address and translate as 'Skandia Hufudhstradkr Maun', or 'Skandia, Howstrake, Mann'

DID YOU KNOW?

My mother once told me
She'd buy me a longship
A handsome-oared vessel
To go sailing with Vikings:
To stand at the stern-post
And steer a fine warship,
Then head back for harbour
And hew down some foemen.

Egil's Saga, chapter 40

---

raised this cross for his soul and that of his brother's wife Gautr made this and all in Man'

land had an advertisement for combs written on it in runes: 'Thorfast made a good comb'. There is even a stone age burial mound at Maeshowe, Orkney which is covered with Viking runic graffiti: 'Haermund Hardaxe carved these runes'.

WHAT HAPPENED TO THE VIKINGS?

The Viking age probably started when the Vikings raided Lindisfarne Abbey in 793, and ended in 1266 when King Magnus IV died. This cannot be exact as Viking rule ended in England in 1066 when it was invaded by William of Normandy, while Shetland and Orkney were still ruled by Norway until 1472. Nevertheless the Vikings ruled large parts of Britian for nearly 500 years. A huge amount can change in that time. For example, 500 years ago Christopher Columbus and others were 'discovering' America, Leonardo da Vince was painting the Mona Lisa and Europeans were drinking coffee for the first time. Talking about 'the Viking age' and expecting it all to be the same all the time is therefore silly. What this book has tried to do is show some of the things the Vikings would have done for some of the time.

What did happen over the years is that the Norsemen stopped going on raids. If raids were 'going viking' (see page 7), then if people stopped raiding they stopped being Vikings. No-one really knows why the raids stopped, just as we're not sure why they started. The Vikings probably stopped raiding partly because they didn't need to – they had already taken whatever land they wanted – and partly because the people they were raiding had organised better defences or moved away from water, so the Vikings couldn't get to them easily in their longships. Basically, raiding was no longer profitable. Besides, the Norsemen had become Christians and Christianity didn't like its followers going around bashing people.

The skills the Vikings brought with them often changed the traditions of the lands they settled however. Manx sod hedges for example (see page 12). They are built using soil and turf on a foundation of stones and are very successful both as windbreaks and as a barrier for livestock. Built properly they last for hundreds of years. They also look remarkably similar to the sort of wall the Vikings built for their longhouses.

Not content with reshaping the land, the Vikings renamed it. Lots of places still have Viking names, including Conister, Injebreck and Kitterland in the Isle of Man, and Holme, Maltby and Thorpe in the UK.

A modern sod hedge, Crowcreen, Maughold, Isle of Man

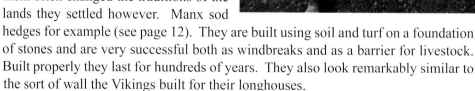

1134
King Olaf I grants Ivo, Abbot of Furness in Cumbria, England, the right to found Rushen Abbey, Malew, Isle of Man

And what about their skill as seafarers? The Viking longships were light, strong, fast and could go almost anywhere there was water. Boatbuilding skills are passed down through families and the style of Viking longships is still recognisable in some modern boats. On Shetland a traditional small fishing boat is the sixareen, an open boat with six oars, and designed so that the six-man crew has an oar each. The shape of the boat is remarkably similar to that of a Viking longship.

But, if the Viking age ended, where did the Vikings go? Well, they didn't go anywhere. Going Viking had never been their main job; they were farmers. They married the people who were already in the lands they conquered and their children knew nowhere else as home. As time went on, few people remembered the difference. If Mary's children had unusually fair hair, or Tom's family had a tradition of calling the eldest daughter Fríðr, well that was just families for you. Their ancestors might originally have come from Scandinavia, but after several centuries they were now Manx, French, English, or even Russian. The Vikings didn't die out. They didn't leave. They're still here.

Left: Odin's Raven *display in the House of Manannan, Peel, Isle of Man.*
Above and right: Far Haaf, *a sixareen named after the Shetland arctic fishing grounds, Unst Boat Haven, Unst, Shetland*

DID YOU KNOW?

Roald Amundsen is sometimes called 'the last Viking'. He was a Norwegian explorer who became the first man to reach the South Pole and the first to go through the 'Northwest Passage', a sea route north of Canada. He died in 1928

A modern Viking warrior looks down from Royalty House, Douglas, Isle of Man

1266
King Magnus IV dies, the Manx crown passes to Alexander III of Scotland, and Norse rule ends in the Isle of Man

ACKNOWLEDGEMENTS

I am indebted to several organisations and individuals who gave up their time to provide help, information and/or photographic material. They include, individuals: Rhonda Cooper, Nicola Didsbury, David Gifford, Sam and his Mum, William Short, Terry Staniforth, Val Turner and Tracy Wood; and organisations: David Gifford Photography, Hurstwic Viking Group, Norsvana Norwegian Forest Cats and Shetland Amenity Trust.

Always of course I am grateful for the support and photographic expertise of my husband, George Hobbs.

Thank you all for your help and assistance; any mistakes are entirely mine.

SELECTED BIBLIOGRAPHY

Bersu, Gerhard, and Wilson, David M., *Three Viking graves in the Isle of Man*, The Society for Medieval Archaeology Monograph Series, No. 1, 1966

Cubbon, W (ed), *The Journal of the Manx Museum Vol IV, No 57*, Manx Museum, December 1938

Jones, Gwyn, *A History of the Vikings*, Oxford University Press, 1969

Loyn, H.R., *The Vikings in Britain*, Book Club Associates, 1977

Magnusson, Magnus, *Vikings!*, BBC, 1992

Martell, Hazel Mary, *Food & Feasts with the Vikings*, Wayland, 1995

Moore, A.W., *The Surnames & Place Names of the Isle of Man*, Elliot Stock, 1890

Page, R.I., *Reading the Past: Runes*, The British Museum, 2001

Parker, Philip, *The Northmen's Fury; a history of the Viking World*, Jonathan Cape, 2014

Sawyer, Peter (ed), *The Oxford Illustrated History of the Vikings*, Oxford University Press, 1997

Various, *The Sagas of Icelanders; a selection*, Penguin Books, 2000

Williams, Gareth, Pentz, Peter, and Wemhoff, Matthias (eds), *Vikings, life and legend*, The British Museum, 2014

Williams, Gareth, *The Viking Ship*, The British Museum, 2014

Wilson, David M., *The Vikings in the Isle of Man*, Aarhus University Press, 2008

Wolf, Kirsten, *Viking Age: everyday life during the extraordinary era of the Norsemen*, Sterling, 2013